EXTREME LIVES

The Shark Man

Written by Laura Valente

Ian Lauder

Ian Lauder likes sharks.
He takes photos of sharks.
His friends call him the shark man.

Q.

How do you stay safe
near the sharks?

A.

I work in a cage.
The cage is tied to a boat.
The sharks can't get in.
But I can take photos.

What do you think Ian does with his shark photos?

3

Q.

How do you get the sharks
to come to you?

A.

I cut up some fish.
The sharks smell the fish's blood
and swim to the cage.

Q.

How do you feel when
you see the sharks come?

A.

I feel scared.
But I know I am safe in the cage.

What sort of tools
do you think
Ian needs to do
his job?

Ian needs special gear
to work under the water.

Blue shark

Q.
What did you do today?

A.
Today, I went down in the cage.
I wanted to see a white shark.
White sharks are very big and scary.

Q.
What did you see?

A.
First I saw a blue shark.
Then a white shark came.
It bit at the cage.
I could see the teeth.
They were very sharp.
I took a photo.

Why do you think
sharks' teeth
are sharp?

7

Q.
How did you feel at the end of the day?

A.
I was happy.
I saw blue sharks and white sharks.
I got lots of great photos.
It was a good day.

Can you find out how many kinds of sharks there are?

White sharks

Hurricane Hunters

Written by Susan Brocker

Hurricane hunters
are very brave.
They are pilots who fly
into dangerous storms
to learn more about them.
The information they get
helps keep people safe.

One day, I went flying
with a hurricane hunter.

The plane was big.
It had lots of computers
and special instruments.

Why do you think
the plane was noisy?

The plane was noisy.
I had to wear earplugs.
The crew had to use headsets
with little microphones
to talk to each other.

The big plane flew into the middle of a storm.
The middle of a storm is called the *eye*.
The wind is not as strong
in the eye of the storm.

The plane flew into the eye four times.
It was like riding a roller coaster.
The plane went up and down.
My stomach felt funny.

The computers and special instruments
on the plane measured the storm.
The information was sent back
to weather forecasters on the ground.
The crew dropped a special instrument
into the storm.
This sent back information, too.

The plane flew for fifteen hours.
I was very tired when we landed.
But I was very happy.
The information we got
helped the weather forecasters.
They could tell how big the storm was.
They could tell where it was going.
They could warn people about the storm.

WEATHER
12360

AIR FORCE

How else
do forecasters
get information for
their weather reports?

The Story of Dian Fossey

Written by Kerrie Capobianco

Dian Fossey read a book
about mountain gorillas.
She liked the book very much.
She wanted to see
the gorillas up close.
So, in 1963, she took
a trip to Africa.

Dian watched
the gorillas
in the wild.
She learned a lot.
Soon, she had to go
home to America.
But she wanted
to learn more.

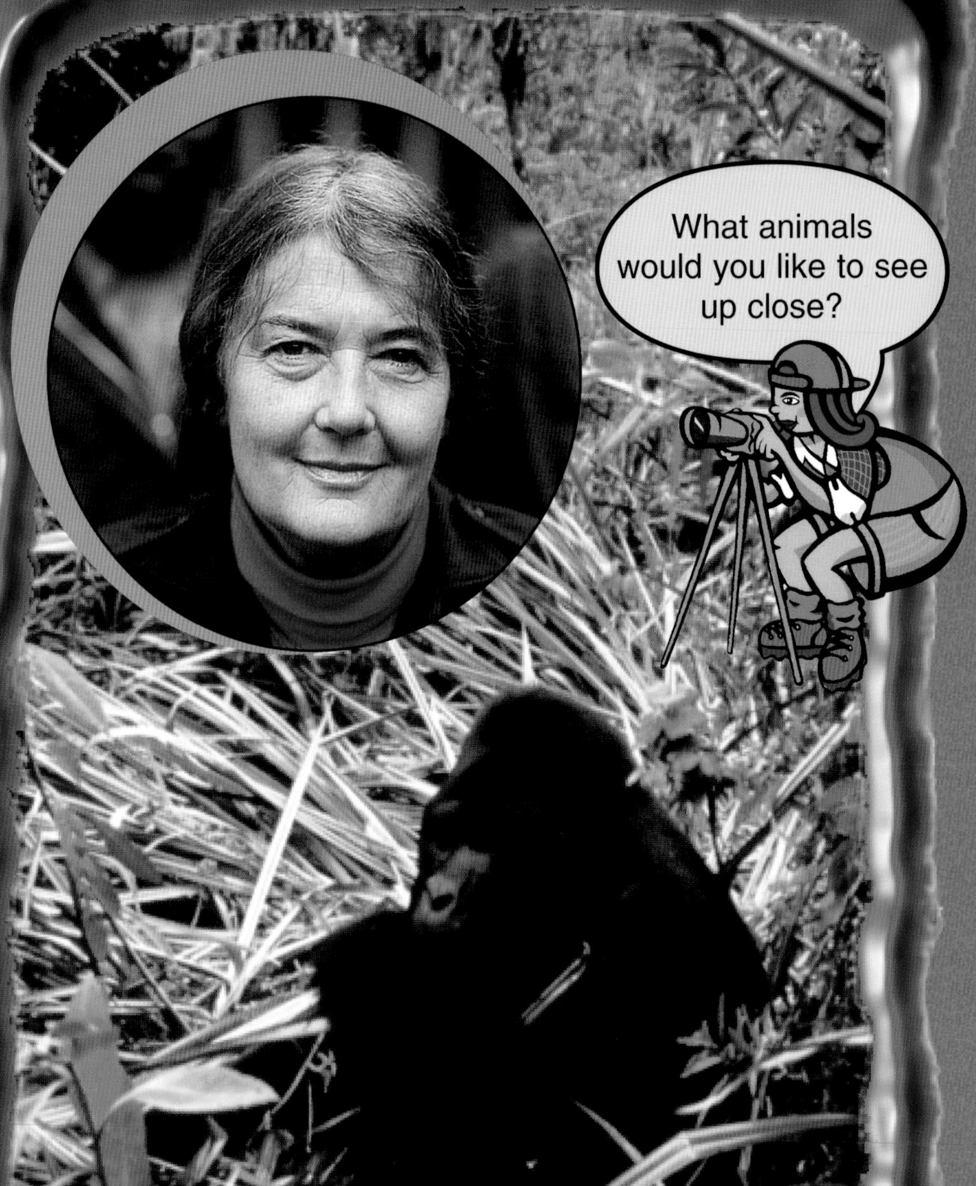
What animals would you like to see up close?

In 1966, Dian Fossey moved to Africa.
She made her home near the gorillas.
She wrote about them
and took photos of them.
She studied them for eighteen years.

Dian learned the gorillas were not safe.
People were hunting gorillas.
They killed some gorillas.
They sold some to zoos.

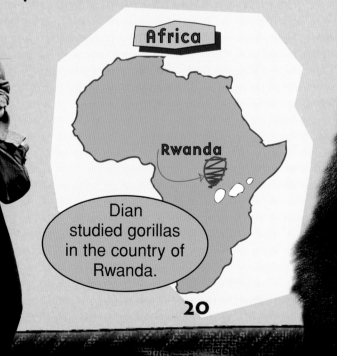

Africa

Rwanda

Dian studied gorillas in the country of Rwanda.

21

Dian wanted to help the gorillas.
So she tried to stop the hunters.
But this made the hunters mad.

In 1985, Dian Fossey was killed.
People think a gorilla hunter killed her.

People know more about the gorillas
because of Dian Fossey.
Today, people are working hard
to help save them.

How could you help the gorillas?

Snake Farm

Written by Claire Roberts

Illustrated by Andrew Leck and Angela Harland

I work on a snake farm.
A snake farm raises snakes.
Some people are scared of snakes.
But I like them.
I even like the poisonous ones.
Why do I like snakes?

Well, when I was a kid,
a poisonous snake bit me.
At the hospital
the doctors gave me a medicine
called antivenin (*ANN tih veh nin*).

It saved my life.
When I grew up,
I got a job at a snake farm.
I wanted to help other people with snake bites.

On the snake farm,
we get poison, or venom,
from snakes.

Some snakes
don't have poison.
How do you think they
kill their prey?

To get the venom,
we hold the snake by its head.
It can't bite us like this.
Then we make it bite
the lid of a jar.
The venom drips into the jar.

We send the venom to scientists.
They use it to make antivenin.
They need lots of venom.

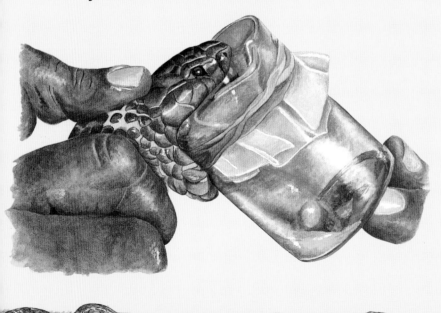

Snake Fangs

A poisonous snake has a gland in its mouth.
This is where the venom is made.
The venom goes down from the gland
into the fangs.

Gland

Some snakes have fangs
at the back of the mouth.
Boomslangs have fangs
like this.

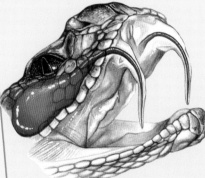

Some snakes have fixed fangs
at the front of the mouth.
Cobras have fangs like this.

Some snakes have folding fangs
at the front of the mouth.
The fangs come out when the
snake opens its mouth.
Vipers have fangs like this.

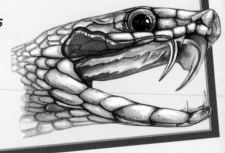

I'm not scared
of being bitten again.
Now I know
how to hold a snake
so it can't bite me.
And if I did get bitten,
I know there's medicine
to help me.

What sort of places
do snakes like
to hide in?

Most snakes
are scared of people.
They only bite if they can't hide.
But if you do get bitten
by a snake,
make sure you know what to do.

Snake Bite First Aid

- Wash the bite
  with clean water and soap.

- Do not move the bitten area
  and keep it lower than the heart.

- If the bite is on the hand or arm,
  remove any rings, watches,
  or tight clothing.

- Get help from a doctor
  as soon as you can.

- If you are a long way from help,
  tie a bandage above the bite.
  The bandage should be loose enough
  to slip a finger under it.

Poisonous Snakes
Around the World

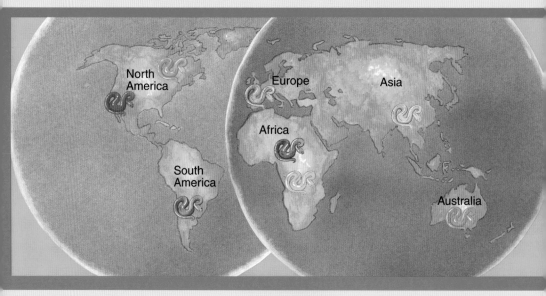

Key

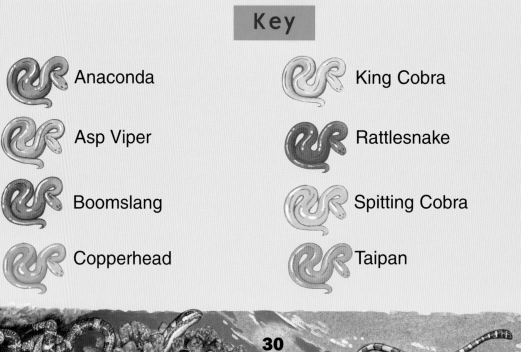

Anaconda

Asp Viper

Boomslang

Copperhead

King Cobra

Rattlesnake

Spitting Cobra

Taipan

Secrets About Snakes

- There are about 2,700 different kinds of snakes in the world.

- Some snakes can live for more than a year without food.

- Snakes don't blink. That's because they don't have any eyelids.

- Snakes use their tongues as well as their nostrils to smell things.

- The most poisonous snake in the world is a kind of sea snake.

- The world's largest poisonous snake is the king cobra. It grows up to 18 feet (5.5 m) long.

Index